THE NEW SCHOOL
OF THE IMAGINATION

Also by JOHN O'MEARA

THE THINKING SPIRIT

THE MODERN DEBACLE

SHAKESPEARE'S MUSE

THE NEW SCHOOL
OF THE IMAGINATION

✦

RUDOLF STEINER'S MYSTERY
PLAYS IN LITERARY TRADITION

John O'Meara

iUniverse, Inc.
New York Lincoln Shanghai

THE NEW SCHOOL OF THE IMAGINATION
RUDOLF STEINER'S MYSTERY PLAYS IN LITERARY TRADITION

iUniverse books may be ordered through booksellers or by contacting:

iUniverse
2021 Pine Lake Road, Suite 100
Lincoln, NE 68512
www.iuniverse.com
1-800-Authors (1-800-288-4677)

ISBN: 978-0-595-46617-7 (pbk)
ISBN: 978-0-595-90912-4 (ebk)

Printed in the United States of America

The author wishes to acknowledge Adam Bittleston, with profound thanks for his superior translation of Rudolf Steiner's Mystery Plays (Rudolf Steiner Press).

Cover Illustration: Sculptural Group by Rudolf Steiner, showing the tall figure of Christ with (to His right, above centre) Lucifer and Ahriman (below). The Goetheanum, Dornach, Switzerland.

Quotations from T.S Eliot's *The Waste Land* from the edition by Faber and Faber.

Contents

During the last decades of the nineteenth-century the Austrian-born RUDOLF STEINER (1861–1925) became a respected and well-published scientific, literary, and philosophical scholar, particularly known for his work on Goethe's scientific writings. After the turn of the century he began to develop his earlier philosophical principles into an approach to methodical research of psychological and spiritual phenomena.

His multi-faceted genius has led to innovative and holistic approaches in medicine, science, education (the Waldorf schools), special education, philosophy, religion, economics, agriculture (the Bio-dynamic method), architecture, drama, the art of eurythmy, and other fields. In 1924 he founded the General Anthroposophical Society, which today has branches throughout the world.

Between 1910 and 1913, Steiner produced four Mystery Plays: *The Portal of Initiation, The Soul's Probation, The Guardian of the Threshold* and *The Souls' Awakening.* The Plays, along with the creation of the art of eurythmy, were part of a general effort to infuse fresh life into Western culture, expressing a new Christian-Rosicrucian inspiration in our time on which Steiner was acting.

Acknowledgments

Once again, to the students of my "Major British Writers" course, given when I was at the University of Toronto.

To Eric Oxford, for his crucial intervention as a reader, which saved this essay from oblivion.

And to Ted Hughes, for his ground-breaking interpretation of Coleridge's unique case, without which also this essay could not have been.

For
Aline Francoeur
my one true thing.

I

I begin from the impasse into which Western literature has fallen, indeed fell as long ago as the twenties of the last century. A continuous line of historical change up to that point (and it is thought, by some, beyond that point) will make it difficult to see that a special leap in evolution is involved, unlike anything before in tradition. It is the leap we have been unable to make, and the consequence has been what I would call the modern stasis: a period that has run its course for almost a hundred years now, marked by a mere repetition of the same modes of progressively worldly consciousness, falling away into manifestations of severe dissociation.

Samuel Beckett took the dramatization of the process of dissociation about as far as it could go. In plays like *Godot* and *Endgame*, he is the anti-Shakespeare of late Western tradition, pursuing the further bottomless route down from tragedy, not the route back up as Shakespeare did in his late plays. Ionesco, in *The Chairs*, brings the process of dissociation to the point of the apocalyptic end of veritable human civilization and of veritable human consciousness. Only a virtual universe remains, in the midst of which Ionesco's protagonists take their final plunge into the annihilation of human consciousness. Both authors knew (as did many others) that the modern and postmodern age could only be seen in the most frightening of terms.

In the meantime a mainstream worldly consciousness carries on to this day in the expression of an effete stoicism, straining after a platitudinous moral propriety. This is the end result of an attitude that cuts itself off from the living tradition of the Imagination and begins, in a more vital artistic form, with Hemingway in the late twenties. Characteristically, in "A Clean, Well-Lighted Place", the hero's whole effort is aimed at sustaining the self-created dignity of his own separate existence artificially maintained in the face of what has become an inchoate universe. The power of Imaginative thinking cannot be extended further, cannot be given further form and content, and the result is that it continually haunts Hemingway's hero from the unconscious and must be severely repressed. In later times, literature declines drastically with this slow, systematic killing off of the Imaginative power in this deeper sense.

The profound creative failure of our time is linked further with the tragedy of the Romantic movement. Brave spirits sought to press forward with their thinking into an otherworld that beckons with possession of the sources of the world's creative forces and of life's meaning. They sought to do so, building on that extraordinary, expansive Soul-power that Wordsworth and Coleridge once defined immemorially as the Imagination. Repulsed in their quest, such spirits were forced back upon a poignant combination of tragic perplexity and resigned faith of the sort Wordsworth experienced when he himself came up against the impasse:

> *The days gone by*
> *Return upon me almost from the dawn*
> *Of life: the hiding-places of man's power*
> *Open; I would approach them, but they close.*
> *I see by glimpses now; when age comes on,*
> *May scarcely see at all; and I would give,*
> *While yet we may, as far as words can give,*
> *Substance and life to what I feel, enshrining,*
> *Such is my hope, the spirit of the Past*
> *For future restoration.*

Wordsworth was not alone in this supreme bafflement. We may claim it also of Coleridge and of Goethe as well as of Yeats and of T.S. Eliot, among many other authors that could be named. I mention these authors here because I am returned to them over the course of my treatment of Rudolf Steiner's Mystery Plays, on account of the tradition of reading from which I emerge. No doubt, other readers will be able to make many other connections. In other work I have presented[1], I have already brought forward the profoundly integral connections that can be claimed among Steiner, Goethe, Coleridge, Emerson and Novalis. And over our epoch as a whole since the Renaissance towers the comprehensive figure of Shakespeare, who went further in Imagination than any latter-day author has ever been, as I have sought to demonstrate elsewhere[2].

What was lacking until Steiner makes his appearance in the late nineteenth-century was a systematically grounded theory of the Imagination. On this basis Steiner would go on to build his overwhelmingly successful venture into the otherworld conducted over the course of many years until his death in 1925. He would become the founder of a new Society among whose membership since then the task has arisen of carrying on with the production of a full-scale culture of the Imagination. To a large extent we are offered a first image of what that Society constitutes among the many characters presented in Steiner's Plays. They comprise among themselves a picture of the first great School of the Imagination in our time. While the modern age is about to take its plunge into a fearful hopelessness, and while the tradition of the Imagination is sputtering to its tragic end, Steiner takes us back *through* that tradition to the point at which the Imagination *ought* to have emerged triumphantly, had the right strength for its further evolution been manifested at the time.

We recall the despair in which Wordsworth, in Bk. XI of *The Prelude*, addresses his lost hopes to Coleridge while the latter was himself convalescing in Malta. The year is 1804; Wordsworth had just produced the "Intimations Ode", his great tragic elegy on the passing away of the Imagination in the primal form he had known. Coinciding with Wordsworth's acknowledgement of his tragic alienation in these terms is Napoleon's self-proclamation as Emperor, in which Wordsworth sees a grotesque correlative of the general "catastrophe" of the time. Wordsworth further invokes the partnership of Coleridge's sad self while the latter was convalescing:

> *To me the grief confined, that thou art gone*
> *....*
> *A lonely wanderer ..., by pain*
> *Compelled and sickness, at this latter day,*
> *This sorrowful reverse for all mankind.*

At this time Coleridge is suffering from the tragic hopelessness of his love for Sara Hutchinson; he is overwhelmed as well by the depth of his poetic inspiration which (unbeknownst to Wordsworth, ironically) Wordsworth had overbearingly repressed in him. In this repressed form, Coleridge's deep inspiration returns to haunt him in horridly fearful ways, to the point where he feels compelled to flee from his inspiration forever[3]. It is the end of English Romanticism in its pure, original phase.

Over in Germany Goethe too had failed, in spite of the grand optimism in which he is expressing himself at this time. Later Goethe, whom we know as the great Sage of Nature, elaborating on a highly penetrating understanding of the interrelationship between Nature and the Mind, and evolving through a progressively greater and greater expansion in poetic consciousness, emerges through what is finally an evasion of the great tragedy of that time, into which he otherwise peers intensely. Years earlier (in 1775) Goethe's Faust had stood himself for a moment before the Spirit of his Imagination, only to find that his strength could not sustain the sudden moment of breakthrough (in the scene "Night. Faust's Study"):

> Faust. (turning away) *O fearful form!*
> Spirit.   *At length*
> *You have compelled me here. Your strength*
> *Has wrestled long about my sphere,*
> *And now—*
> Faust. *I tremble: come not near.*
> Spirit. *With bated breath you laboured to behold me,*
> *To hear my voice, to see me face to face.*
> *You prayed with might, with depth that has controlled me,*
> *And here I am—What horror now can chase*
> *The colour from your lips, my superman?*
> *Where the soul's cry? The courage that began*
> *To shape a world, and bear and foster it?*
> *The heart that glowed, with lofty ardour lit,*
> *To claim ethereal spirits as your peers?*
> *Are you that Faust whose challenge smote my ears,*
> *Who beat his way to me, proclaimed his hour,*
> *And trembles now in presence of my power,*
> *Writhes from the breath of it, a frightened worm?*
> *...*
> *You match the spirit that you comprehend,*
> *Not me. (He vanishes)*

Faust goes on to draw an agreement with Mephistopheles on the basis that, having failed to penetrate to the otherworldly sources of his Imagination, he can only give himself to all that drives a human soul in its perpetual restlessness—the sphere of merely sensual existence (however grand in spirit) to which Mephistopheles freely opens the door. Goethe does not seem to have grasped Faust's condition in these terms until he sat down to write the agreement-scene over twenty-two years later in 1797. He was building, on the other hand, on a view of his hero's sensual destiny that he had already grasped well in 1786 when he paints a Faust who knows precisely what he stands for in the comparison with Margaret:

> *Do I not know myself to be her doom?*
> *I, the uprooted, I the homeless jade,*

The monster I, whose only aim is this:
To scour the rocks like any blind cascade
Racing and eager for the dark abyss.

...

And I, the curse of God upon my brow,
I, not content
To grip the rocks and make them bow
And leave them rent,
Must undermine her innocence as well,
And make of her a sacrifice for Hell!

In spite of the threat he poses, Faust *will* make a sacrifice of Margaret, unable to endure his dilemma, and Goethe will take us through what is perhaps the most distressing tragedy in late Western European tradition. In the last scene of Part One, Faust will penetrate Margaret's prison cell unable to entice her away from her certain death and ultimate social opprobrium, which he has brought upon her.

At only one other point (besides the early *Faust*) does Goethe return to the issue, though with a success on which he could not have counted, since he remained only half-conscious of his venture and would not pursue the matter further. He returns to it in his great "Tale of the Green Snake and the Beautiful Lily", written around 1795. Here Goethe suddenly, and almost haphazardly, invests the Youth with precisely the capacity that had eluded Faust up to that point—the capacity of "dying into" otherworldly Powers that further the Imagination in its being. It is the moment in Western European tradition to which Steiner returns in his Plays, to carry on with the task of helping with the further emergence of the Imagination in our time. Steiner's Johannes—the main hero to whom we are introduced in the first play—is based directly on Goethe's Youth, his extraordinary course of growth in the Imagination moving along the very same lines. It is not an easy growth, as Goethe himself knew well, for it proceeds through a profound assumption of guilt, of the sort that Goethe's Faust evades. Challenged to direct spirit-knowledge by the initiate leader of this School—who bears the name of Benedictus—Johannes finds himself abandoning the value of his temporal being (as an artist among other things) and, consequently, experiences an appalling emptiness through which the voice of one he has betrayed returns to haunt him as her murderer. This voice could well be that of Margaret from Goethe's *Faust* (the echo appears to be intentional):

> *"He brought me bitter need.*
> *I gave him all my trust.*
> *He left me in my misery alone.*
> *He robbed me of the warmth of life*
> *and drove me into the cold earth."*

The act of self-emptying leaves a void in Johannes in which at first nothing else is experienced *except for* the voice that proclaims his guilt to him. Beyond this experience, Johannes is confronted further exclusively with the essence of his lust and greed, which appears to him, out of the abyss of his being, in the form of a revolting dragon:

> *Knowledge chains me to you, you destroying monster.*

Faust comes as far as to see the monster in himself but is otherwise unable to confront himself. Post-Romantic experience is emphatically defined by this inability to confront guilt in the self in the pure form and to the extreme extent that was required. The consequence of this avoidance, paradoxically, would be the great ravagement by *uncomprehended* guilt that subsequently pervades the course of the nineteenth and early twentieth centuries, leaving nothing but terror and waste in its wake.

English literary experience points the historical impasse rather sharply. The Protestant angst of being fallen in the self, which at a certain point overtakes all the major authors of post-Reformation England (from Marlowe and Shakespeare right through to Milton) strangely enough has disappeared by the time we reach Wordsworth's efforts to link the self directly to Nature and to the Imagination. New forces of Nature and of the Imagination have spontaneously emerged in their own right, but there would be no successful attempt to relate these emergent forces back to the question of inalienable guilt that had so occupied an earlier age. Milton's whole endeavour consisted in the faith that he had come, in the epic grandeur of his Republican cause, to offer an historical solution to human depravity, which, like everyone else in the post-Reformation age, he took to be the first condition of human nature. Milton, as we know, was dramatically defeated in this attempt and in defeat strikes a figure that compares poignantly with the figure of the ailing Coleridge that Wordsworth invokes as an image of their common condition by 1804. Indeed, between the age of Shakespeare and of Milton, on the one hand, and that of Wordsworth, on the other, lies an abiding abyss, and it is tragic but fitting that Coleridge and Wordsworth both should be returned to that abyss by 1804 when Wordsworth is himself dramatically admitting the defeat of the Imagination.

In the meantime, in a strong tradition of moral engagement—between the towering figures of Swift on the one hand and Blake on the other, the fact that the abyss was *not* being plumbed is just what human society was being excoriated for. "How morally and imaginatively small humanity is!", we seem to hear them saying. Swift would never cease to call his readers' attention to the intolerable smallness of their moral natures, the hopeless incapacity humanity showed for experiencing moral shame, while at the other end of the scale, Blake would for years bewail, unheard, the pathetically small use humanity was making of its imaginative potential, incapable as he supposed humanity to be of any shame over the smallness of its imaginative ideas. Lacking was any proper understanding of the necessary intercorrespondence between the two orders that linked the further emergence of the Imagination with a full encounter with the depravity in human nature that remained.

Johannes in the opening of *The Portal of Initiation* confronts the depth of *his* depravity with a degree of exclusiveness and a completeness that, in late European literature, is unique. A further progress in Imagination becomes uniquely available to him as a result of the extreme nature and degree of the engagement that is acted on. Johannes undergoes this experience in the company of a fully emergent and well-founded School. Hence the figure of Maria, who comes to meet Johannes in the depths of his terror, bearing the faith that there is a purpose to Johannes's suffering:

> *You must experience every terror*
> *to which illusion can give birth*
> *before the truth reveals itself to you:*
> *thus speaks your star.*

Benedictus explains how at one point he had to help with the ensoulment of

> *.... that Spirit*
> *who should be given power to work*
> *now through our human world.*

Steiner's research as a whole identifies this Spirit as *Anthropos-Sophia*—the traditional Sophia who, since the Renaissance, now works directly in and through Man.[4] Benedictus's choice for the ensoulment of this Spirit in our time is Maria, who, consequently, mediates the Power by which one emerges into an otherworld of the Imagination in a way that is *fully* conscious. Working, as she does, purely in this way, Maria must first convert those who become involved with her from all that continues to bind their interest to the temporal world, all of which must now appear as perversion. Thus Johannes has had to confront, in the purest and most direct terms, the full extent of *his* share in human perversion, in the form of the dragon of lust and greed that confronts him early on as the essence of his nature. Benedictus acknowledges the extraordinary self-preservation Johannes has shown when faced with the forces of destruction that have sought to overcome him:

> *My son, you have preserved your self,*
> *when....*
> *.... wrapped in terror ...;*
> *Your self has strongly battled through*

Benedictus lets Johannes know that from the time he had shown a power of engaging the abyss, the Initiate was there to offer Johannes a further strength to hold himself together:

> *Truly you have been my pupil since that hour*
> *when you were near despair about yourself,*
> *and took yourself for lost,*
> *and yet the strength within you still held firm.*
> *I was allowed to give from wisdom's treasures*
> *what brought you strength to hold yourself*
> *though you believed no longer in yourself.*

And from Benedictus, Johannes now discovers that he must seek Maria in the Spirit-regions to which she momentarily ascends. But the circumstances of the ascent are frightful. Johannes must witness Maria's spiritual separation from the temporal part of her that remains behind, in Johannes's full view, demonically possessed:

> *But who is speaking?*
> *I do not see Maria,*
> *I see a ghastly being.*

Having preserved himself in the abyss, Johannes is given the privilege "to look on spirit-being consciously", even if this be, at first, but another harsh trial, since Johannes gazes only upon the demonic counterpart to Maria's higher self:

> *and you, my son, have seen the temporal part*
> *of her to whom your love streams out entire,*
> *drop into darkness.*
> *Since often through her mouth*
> *the spirits spoke to you,*
> *world Karma has not spared you*
> *from hearing through her too*
> *the prince of hell.*[5]

In the presentation of Geraldine in "Christabel", one likewise finds the psychic reflection of an activity illuminating the demonic basis of the inner quest. On the verge of his own spirit-breakthrough, Coleridge breaks down and withdraws: apart from Coleridge's own doubts in the face of demonic manifestation, Wordsworth made sure Coleridge considered nothing more of the sort.[6] However, advancement in spirit-knowledge would seem to presuppose some such direct encounter with those demonic powers in the world that seek to pervert or distract from spirit-growth, especially through terror of them in their primal manifestations. In a certain portion of itself, though in a way that is unpremeditated, the individual spirit finds the further "strength" that sees it through "to look on spirit-being consciously". Johannes's success in this respect grows out of his longstanding experience (of ten years) in the School and is inconceivable outside that experience. All that follows depends strictly on Johannes finding this primordial "strength" of which Steiner's Plays speak. Elsewhere in Steiner's work, in his actual preparation of the School his plays allude to, we find a detailed account of the process by which Johannes comes to this point of unfolding "strength".[7]

At issue is the kind of "strength" to which Coleridge aspired and which he distinguished from the mere prophetic "power" he possessed, an impressive faculty in its own right but one he knew was insufficient to allow for the kind of breakthrough into spirit-worlds he could anticipate.[8] Johannes has been tested further and found ready to be "released out of the world of sense". Unflinchingly he looks upon horrible spirit-representations of obstructive perversion in himself, and thereby comes to distinguish between the mere temporal part of his existence by which he is misled (the consequence of his devoting himself so entirely to Maria in the flesh) and his actual, genuine spiritual direction, which Maria now represents to him purely, out of the "spirit-heights" to which her soul retires. Into these heights Johannes himself now ventures, very largely because of the direction Benedictus feels justified in offering him:

> *Now it is right that you should seek her*
> *and learn to know her innermost being.*
> *And she shall represent for you*
> *that higher human being*
> *toward which you shall raise yourself.*
> *Her soul is hovering in the spirit heights*
> *where men can find their being's archetype,*
> *which is sustained within itself.*
> *Follow her now into the spirit region,*
> *....*
> *My son, since you have held yourself so far,*
> *you will reach further.*

II

The deeper challenge facing Johannes comes from the situation in which he is placed when his hidden lust for Maria is revealed to him. In "Christabel", Coleridge also grasped the lust in his love for Sara Hutchinson (frustrated as this love was by his marriage), which he too saw as a grotesquely violent attack on what was most holy.[9] Coleridge also understood that great forces of self-knowledge lay hidden in such a revelation, and that it devolved upon him to *confront* this secret aspect of his nature, but he would be unable to explore the matter any further. Self-knowledge is given to Johannes through the dreadful appearance of the demon of his Double in whom this lust continues to be morbidly dramatized. His Double thus continues to drive Johannes, in spite of his resistance, into deeper and deeper spheres of the knowledge of himself. Even in his perverse spirit, Johannes recognizes what his Double is capable of doing for him:

> *O likeness of my being, you have shown*
> *yourself till now before me with the purpose*
> *of making me appalled at my own self.*
> *I understand about you still but little;*
> *and yet I recognize that it is you*
> *who guides my soul. You are the hindrance*

against my free existence, and the reason
I do not comprehend my own true being.

The perversity in Johannes consists in pretending that his sensual dependency on Maria is inevitable and that he remains free to express himself in this nature even in the inner quest. He is even led fallaciously to suppose that such sensuality must serve as the basis for that quest. Likewise later Yeats will make as much of the subjection to the sensual self (and its "bitterness" and "violence") as the need for creation is felt. Implied in this development, however, is the acceptance of atavism, and it is a measure of the psychological risk involved in the turn inwards, which is otherwise inevitable.

To Ted Hughes it seemed clear that while Coleridge was in possession of the deeper turn inwards, he stood poised, exceptionally among the English Romantics, to tap into a comprehensive, "holistic"[10] basis for Imagination. This basis, Hughes speculates, has to do with what he calls "the deity of the blood-stream"[11], which is how Coleridge expressly represents it. In this way, Coleridge is judged to be another D.H. Lawrence before his time, for whom "the Serpent Power" behind his figure of the "Serpent Woman", or the awakening of Kundalini, was his true subject, though he fled from it in dismay.[12] Whatever we may think of this as a final reading of Coleridge, the question remains how this Power is to be tapped into, for it would appear to involve at every turn a struggle of great moment, with a way through that is far from being assured, or for that matter, very straightforward at all.

That which Hughes suggests Coleridge ought to have celebrated as "the river of life" represented *in* the "blood stream" in Lawrence presupposes a tremendous struggle first with what *he* called "the river of dissolution", from which there was no great assurance of coming free.[13] Coleridge is himself much embroiled in this "river of dissolution", as Hughes's account of him superabundantly makes clear. What we might describe as Lawrence's emphatic, first (or primordial) "river" signifies, in fact, all those dangerous ensnarements of the passion and of the blood that he was very clear have always stood in wait upon the inward journey, and which would have to be very wisely circumvented before one could even *begin* to transcend and come free. We are returned in this way to the immoveable problem of lust and greed with which Johannes is found grappling from the beginning. Not that there is another way to come *fully* "to the light" than by means of such an in-depth inward engagement with one's sensual nature, or one would have to forego all human warmth in the process. Only it will be seen that the "blood" is bound, in the nature of the case, continually to confound, short of a

greater perfecting of our nature. Hence, there *must* be the further help of a gratuitous dispensation that allows one to be "brought to the light" *in the midst of one's
sensual nature.* Such illumination takes place even as one ensures that no
encroachments of that nature are allowed to interfere with the purity or truthful-
ness of the illuminating process.[14]

◆   ◆   ◆

The very great gift of the Anthroposophical School of Initiation in our time
consists precisely in its act of support and bestowal of gratuitous illumination,
even while the further struggle with our sensual natures continues. It is the lesson
that Johannes himself derives from the long course of instruction in which he is
directed by the powers that have taken his Initiation in hand:

> *Spirit-pupilship*
> *has granted me a Self which can be strong*
> *and can unfold its own creative work*
> *although its bearer has to know himself*
> *far from the highest purposes of souls.*
> *In this condition, when he has the duty*
> *to devote this second man awakened in him*
> *to earthly evolution—always must he*
> *let shine as his most earnest rule of life*
> *before his spirit's sight, that he must never*
> *let anything that comes from his own self*
> *enter disturbingly the work done not by him*
> *but by his second self.* [15]

To reach this point of deeper self-understanding, Johannes must depend on the
process of Initiation itself to set him right. Even his Double is confounded for a
time, until the Guardian of the Threshold intervenes to expose the basis of
Johannes's sensual drive in his love of himself. This self-love has had a profoundly
disturbing effect on his Imagination, and another great spiritual Power is in this
way highlighted to us that clearly bears a tremendous influence on the whole process.

◆   ◆   ◆

All that Johannes gains exceptionally in the way of an *outer* content from his journey into himself is to be set down to a Power that Steiner explains is the one that more and more must be tapped into, if we are indeed to have further success with the Imaginative process. Here, however, it must be clearly established that the candidate for Initiation is first supported by a School that carries in itself the seeds for a successful negotiation with this Power. Otherwise, there is the danger of succumbing precisely to confusion of the sort Coleridge sensed about himself. Thus Johannes enlists the further help required to keep the illuminating Power in check, even while *it* proceeds to offer the necessary basis for an outer content to the Imaginative process. Fittingly it is Maria who expounds on the nature of that Power, who is none other than the Serpent Power, Lucifer. He it is who now makes outward, from the place he has always held deep in the inwardness of the human soul, that part of the Imaginative process in which human beings directly participate by virtue of their free role on earth, which will always ensure their individuality in that process:

> *When he as bringer of the light streams out*
> *his wisdom, filling worlds with his proud sense*
> *of selfhood, splendid as example*
> *of individuality to every being*
> *in his bold self-assertion—then*
> *the inwardness of human souls may bring*
> *itself into appearance, with delight,*
> *and joy in wisdom, spreading round itself*
> *what loves to live and find itself in life.*

The danger with this individual basis to the Imagination, however, lies in the temptation to project oneself into Lucifer's Power by partaking *with him* in this creation, who otherwise has his basis in the sensual nature:

> *So man may turn to Lucifer to feel*
> *warm joy at splendour and at beauty:*
> *through this man may experience himself*
> *yet not with Lucifer as his own being.*

And *that* danger remains constant:

> *And yet man's soul will always wish*
> *to **waken** in itself, what it should only*
> ***look on** with wonder. It should see*
> *Lucifer's beauty, but not fall*
> *into his power, so that he*
> *can do his will within it.*

The consequence of such an implicit act of identification must be the further breakdown into sensual degradation that drastically clogs the nature of those who once partake in the Imaginative ideal Lucifer awakens. That ideal is simultaneously curtailed in its expression, dispossessed at that point of any further potential for opening outwardly to revelation. The effects of that degradation are now themselves projected in place of the outer ideal that has failed to fully manifest. For one who is not *made* to see, however, it will continue to appear as if the possibilities of power for the personality remain endless—opening up the frightful prospect, through clairvoyant vision, of a form of domination over others that history has yet to see but might one day see (nor do Steiner's Plays show this to us). It is a form of domination in which the presiding personality would remain *un*aware of its immersion in ever-deepening degradation, the infinite extension of which would be that personality's love of itself driving every other personality away before it.

III

Of crucial significance is the challenge posed by the problem of holding *together* in "strength" in that extraordinary moment when the action of spirit-growth first makes itself felt. In Johannes's case, the problem is highlighted in the form of the overwhelming terror of being destroyed in his ego, from his helpless participation in the vision of his demonic nature. Capesius, another character with whom Johannes is linked, undergoes a significantly different experience, in *The Soul's Probation. His* terror is of losing himself to a sudden expansiveness in the spirit, without the support of *any* knowledge of his ego, which he has hitherto exclusively identified with his historical-cultural practice as a scholar. In Johannes we see the ready expansiveness of the artist who, in spite of his good will, continues to be confounded by his sensual attachment to the world (the burden of the late-nineteenth-century artist generally). In Capesius (the embodiment of post-

Renaissance humanistic scepticism) we identify the intellectual eminence that, for all its success in historical-cultural terms, cannot provide a form of knowledge that can match up to the prospect of spirit vision—even after Capesius recognizes the indispensable necessity of such vision.[16]

This compounded predicament—highlighting the spiritual anguish of the artist/poet, on the one hand, and the cultural-historical scholar, on the other—T.S. Eliot would fix upon, ten-to-fifteen-years later, in the transition from *The Waste Land* to *Ash-Wednesday*. Like Eliot the scholar, infusing his despairing consciousness into the poetic fabric of *The Waste Land*, Capesius tormentedly acknowledges the illusory nature of *his* intellectual-cultural constructs, which, for all their success in worldly cultural terms, leave him imprisoned in a condition of spiritual ignorance:

> *Through my whole life, I only wove in pictures*
> *that form as shadows in the dreaming soul*
> *as, in its prison of illusion,*
> *it mirrors nature and the works of spirit,*
> *trying to solve the riddles of the world*
> *in spectral fashion with its web of dreams.*[17]

Trying to respond to the exhortation he receives from Benedictus, to know himself in spiritual terms, Capesius can fathom only the collapse of his former world, with something of that suggestion of being left both spiritually airless and in terror that is a strong effect in Eliot's poem:

> *It is as if breath leaves me,*
> *when I attempt to grasp[his] words.*
> *Before I feel what I should think, appalling fear takes hold of me.*
> *It seems as if all the surroundings*
> *I had in life till now, were crashing round me,*
> *destroying me among their ruins.*

Confronting his own nothingness, Capesius is then overtaken by a vision of powers of soul that obtrude upon him from a deeper Self whose basis terrifies him by its indeterminacy. He is without a sense of his own self in meeting this deeper entity. His experience at this point is precisely the one Eliot, in his lectures on *The Use of Poetry and the Use of Criticism*, would claim haunted Coleridge, insinuating by his reference a similar experience of his own.[18] Steiner's representation lays bare the frightening immediacy of the experience:

> *I felt just now, as if my Self had fled*
> *to depths of worlds, and powers strange to me*
> *were speaking through the organs of the Self*
> *here in this room.*

Capesius's challenge lies in finding a way in which to support himself in the face of this sudden deepening in spirit, as Benedictus explains:

> *For you have come into a realm*
> *that must remain illusion for you*
> *so long as in it you still lose yourself;*
> *but which will open the first gates*
> *of every wisdom for you*
> *when you preserve yourself within it.*

Capesius, as the type of the humanistic scholar, turns out to be a victim of his own hopefulness, disposed to *over*credit the value of man's accomplishments in the world, in relation to the spirit. He can only see the possibilities of cultural achievement for man, must compulsively refer any possible language of the spirit to man's language, since for him this is the all-in-all. This disposition of humanistic hopefulness must fail Capesius when he finally plunges into the actual realities of spirit, which demand a purer, less self-concerned and so less vulnerable sense of identity. His position compares directly with that of Eliot who, in the beginning of *Ash Wednesday*, looks upon the renunciation of his cultural-poetical self as his only hope if he is to progress further in the spirit. The effort to preserve himself, after renouncing every attachment to the world both scholarly and poetic, will lead Eliot to those tremendous involutions of self-searching that characterize his progression through the many parts of *Ash-Wednesday*, where he lays claim to his own understanding and experience of supportive worlds.

Before that happens, however, Eliot will have to contend with yet another side of his spiritually beleaguered self, about which we may gather insight from a *third* character in Steiner's compound picture of the many forms of present-day cultural-scientific knowledge. This is Strader (the type of post-Renaissance sceptical science). *His* will be the dire problem of *not*-knowing (in the most radically dispossessed sense) when his notions of the spirit as illusion are contradicted by the effects of spirit everywhere around him. Strader remains without the slightest inkling as to how to penetrate to the sources of such spirit:

> *My destiny has not allowed*
> *that any ray of hope*
> *for this defeated life*
> *should reach my heart.*

When associated with Johannes and Capesius, Strader represents, as it were, the *other* side of that all-encompassing need Eliot identifies in *Ash-Wednesday* as the elusive and tantalizing "strength beyond hope *and despair*". Along the way, Eliot would find *his* support by embracing the spiritual offerings of Church tradition—reaching back to sources in late medieval tradition—in the monumental figure of his "Lady", who has the power to intercede on his behalf. On this point too we find a parallel in Steiner's play in the consolations of a graceful life that come upon Strader as the result of his later marriage to the seeress, Theodora.

◆   ◆   ◆

Capesius's weakness stems from fear. Remaining bound to his cultural-intellectual identity, he continues in fear of what the spirit-world has to reveal about the self-transformation he must undergo. Capesius fears what the spirit-world has to think out with him, because it points to purposes other than those supposed by the idle projections men *take* for cultural-intellectual thinking, which he now perceives as mere "weightless dreams":

> *Fear and bewilderment would come upon them*
> *if they could learn how spirits guide the course*
> *of being, as they will.*

As in Johannes's case, Maria is sent to help Capesius. She makes him see what is another side to the spirit-reality with which the new spirit-culture must contend. She shows him that his fear derives from an excess of thinking involved in the form of cultural-intellectual thinking he has always practised, which in an interfering way translates the expectation of the revelation of spirit-purposes into fear. This particular form of setback is presented as the effect of the other main confounding Power in the process of spirit-growth, operating on the other side of Lucifer, yet intimately associated with him, and identified to us as Ahriman. *He* it is who connects us to the outer world in our thinking, but as confounding Power, he pretends to extend that same thinking into the spirit-world, as if *it* could be appropriated *by* the outer. It is thus to Ahriman and his purposes that we owe the threat of another form of material perversion of spirit-purposes, leading to yet another form of debased culture. Ahriman's purposes are seen (in Scene VI of *The Guardian of the Threshold*) to derive from a time when the Creation might have belonged to the joint control of Lucifer and himself, before the Gods who *are* the world's Creators, and rule with spirit-purposes of their own, proceeded to assume their own control of human destiny on earth, consigning Ahriman

> *from their kingdom to the depths*
> *of the abyss—that I might not*
> *give **too much** strength to men.*

> *Thus only from this place can I*
> *send to the earth strong power.*
> *But on this path it turns to—Fear.*

Capesius must dissociate from the ideal of thinking Ahriman continues to impose upon him, which may be suitable for taking hold of the world's realities in their cultural-material expressions but is otherwise unsuitable for grasping the deeper spirit-purposes those realities were intended to serve. Because Capesius cannot dissociate himself from this familiar form of thinking, he is unable to progress further in spirit-purposes; he remains stuck in a power of spirit-vision that merely "sees", without further power to affect or to take forward, unable to begin to transform himself. Until, from the gratuitous influence of Maria and Benedictus both, having been deemed inwardly worthy of this help, Capesius is led a little further along. He is brought to the point of perceiving how he can at least begin to effect a breakthrough, beyond the arresting fear that is holding up his development for now. He is painfully learning how to open to thoughts from spirit-worlds that originate from a source outside his own thinking. The debilitating effects of his own crippling power of thinking are at the same time *also* outwardly revealed to him in this further process of illumination, as Benedictus explains:

> *For he alone*
> *who learned to see outside himself his thinking,*
> *as powers of seership can perceive*
> *the earthly body separate from them,*
> *enters the spirit's full realities.*

And so behold in picture, that through powers
of seership then the picture may be changed
to knowledge for thee—thoughts, which make
themselves to living forms in space
mirroring human thinking.

What is then acted out before Capesius's Imaginative sight is a highly elaborate view of how the forces of Lucifer and Ahriman, from their respective sides, are combining in him. It is the direct influence of these Powers that is revealed to Capesius in this moment. Johannes for his part seeks, misguidedly, to unite with Lucifer out of the depths of the whole personality, though he has not attained to the full purity that alone would make this possible. Contrastingly, we see how Lucifer draws Capesius into a strictly mental involvement with the power of spirit-seeing, while on the other side Ahriman continues to insist on the kind of counter-thinking that forces Capesius to separate from his personality in fear—fear of the dire effects this thinking is having on him in the spirit-world. Freedom from fear lies in the power to see that fear outside oneself, as the creation of Someone other than who one is, and with that revelation a more promising prospect lies ahead for Capesius:

And since you could behold outside yourself
what you have dreamt as your own being—
now find yourself; do not draw back in fear

◆   ◆   ◆

Finally there is the case of Strader, dispossessed for the moment of *any* insight into Luciferic spirit-revelation. *He* can only be helped into a sense of spirit by his marriage to Theodora who, more than any other character in these Plays, is gifted with spirit-revelation. He is more deeply caught than is Capesius in the Ahrimanic thinking that has him bound, to the point of a complete darkening of spirit-experience; this is until the appearance of Theodora, from whom Strader hears intimately of her experience:

You let me learn in such a way
of what the higher worlds revealed to you
that every doubt could quickly disappear.

In their further union in marriage, Strader lives in a kind of atmosphere of spirit-revelation around her that works to transform his thinking. In the midst of his life as a scientist, among machinery, he sees the possibility of working the Spirit into the human activity such machinery dictates. He is even brought to the point of inventing a new form of machinery, such as will allow human activity at this level in future to conform with spirit-aims:

> *even machinery*
> *which I now serve, I was allowed to feel*
> *as capable of being fertilised*
> *by those who bear themselves towards the Spirit*
> *rightly. It was the spiritual power*
> *which you could give me, helping on my life,*
> *that let me see the interplay of forces*
> *in such a way that the invention*
> *could stand before my spirit suddenly*
> *as if I was inspired—of this, it seems,*
> *much may be hoped.*

Under the further influence of Benedictus, Strader finds himself directly transported in spirit, not to the blessed realm of Lucifer as he had hoped, but to the dark, forbidding realm of Ahriman, from which it is the task of Strader especially to learn. There he comes to realize that in someone like himself a spiritual use can be made even of the Ahriman-thinking, inasmuch as spirit-purposes encompass and relate to *all* worlds. It would be a matter, out of a consciousness of the existence of these purposes, of his bringing himself and others into a further proper relationship to the *outer* workings of the universe. For the same spirit-order is reflected also in the outer arrangement of universal happenings, as Benedictus explains:

> *The powers of the cosmos guide their deeds*
> *in such a way that they accord*
> *with measure and with number, and unite*
> *wisely with the becoming of all worlds.*
> *The sign of the fulfilment of this order*
> *is clearly shown to the external senses*
> *when they observe the Sun as it pursues*
> *its course through the twelve figures of the stars.*

As it relates to these
so things on earth through ages come about.

IV

Johannes, Capesius and Strader, all three, must think of working at still more evolved relationships among themselves in the future, for they represent the three main tendencies in the human personality that are ultimately to be brought into order. As Benedictus explains (in Scene X of *The Guardian of the Threshold*), as long as the different components of the human personality are operating separately, "being" will be achieved but not that further unfolding "life" out of which a future culture of the Imagination can spring. Finding a true basis for the workings of the Imagination in the future involves, first, clarification about an inescapable encounter with Lucifer; into this will then be brought, with time, a further use of Ahriman's influence, when the human personality finds, beyond its bearings in the spiritual world, its further, full "alignment" with the workings of the outer universe. That latter prospect lies far ahead in the future; in the meantime, the greater part of the emphasis must fall, as it does in Steiner's Plays, on the nature of that first encounter with Lucifer, upon which, in the first full bringing together of all forces concerned, in the Rosicrucian School of Scene X of *The Guardian of the Threshold*, Maria expounds climactically (in the passages I have quoted above.)

At this point, we see what to make of a struggle of the kind Coleridge went through, who found himself overwhelmed by Lucifer, to the point of a terrible distortion in himself of the Goddess-influence that Ted Hughes shows was also at work in him. In Steiner's Plays, Maria reflects the Spirit of that Goddess in Her *true* influence, which takes place in our time. In her we see how and why, today, one is *not* to fear in the encounter with Lucifer. No longer need the overwhelming influence of Lucifer be what it once was or can still be. Coleridge retreated before that influence into his superintellectualized abstraction (to become, by default, the greatest theorist of the Imagination in English tradition), but in his repressed passionate life all converted to inner nightmare. He lingers out his life in the midst of such intense complications as the most profoundly visited of English poets, as we shall see further.

Eliot, for his part, was ready to do more than merely suspend *his* Ahrimanic cultural-intellectual thinking. In *Ash-Wednesday* he struggles to renounce such thinking altogether, just as he also works at abandoning Luciferic self-love. These are the twin conditions (corresponding to the shared struggle between Capesius and Johannes) Eliot knew he *had* to transcend, to achieve any further authentic progress in spirit-vision. His struggle with himself in the meantime compares directly with the liberating effort Capesius makes, at a different level, to envision the fearful effects of continued temptation outside himself, as in the third section of Eliot's poem:

> *At the first turning of the second stair*
> *I turned and saw below*
> *The same shape twisted on the banister*
> *Under the vapour in the fetid air*
> *Struggling with the devil of the stairs who wears*
> *The deceitful face of hope and of despair.*[19]

Eliot was not operating with the advantage of the Anthroposophical revelation of our time, and consequently his effort is not transposed directly to the sphere of spirit-vision, but in his spiritual disposition—struggling against the idealizations of self-love and of cultural-intellectual thinking both—he is clearly moving in that direction. Eliot strenuously directs himself in the new centring influence of his poem's "Lady" who, mediating the refining power of the Goddess as "Mother", gathers to herself the "white light" of grace out of which Eliot's spiritual progress is shaped. This "white light" re-appears in full splendor in the second section of "Burnt Norton", where it takes on more openly the significance of the Word of which it bears witness. The same central significance is assigned to the Christ in Steiner's Anthroposophy but on the basis of a full reckoning with the Christian-Rosicrucian stream. Eliot stands in relation to the accomplishment represented in Steiner's Plays in fact very much as did the medieval mystics to the Rosicrucian initiates who appear just beyond their time. As Rudolf Steiner explains, the mystics made themselves "*ready* to be led as ... Rosicrucian initiate[s] ... into those regions which ... may now be called the Luciferic worlds."[20]; they made themselves ready by allowing the soul to be "gradually permeated by the spiritual substance of the Christ, ... cleansed and purified ..."[21]. *Their* progress ended at that point, but Steiner also indicates that "As soon as the Christ has worked in the soul for a while, the soul, permeated by the Christ substance, *becomes mature enough to penetrate again* into the realm of the Luciferic beings." And this "[t]he Rosicrucian initiates were the first to be able to do ..."[22]

Maria herself stands at the centre of such an Initiation when, adding to her account of Lucifer, she says:

> *Yet men, more than all other spirits,*
> *are needy of that God, who does not only*
> *claim wonder when he is revealed*
> *in outer being, glorious to the soul—*
> *but only shows His highest power*
> *when dwelling in the inwardness of souls;*
> *He who proclaims with love the life in death.*
> *So man may turn to Lucifer to feel*
> *warm joy at splendour and at beauty:*
> *through this man may experience himself*
> *yet not with Lucifer as his own being.*
> *But to the other Spirit man may cry*
> *when he can rightly comprehend himself:*
> *it is the loving purpose of earth's soul:*
> *not I, but Christ, is living in my being.*

Among the genuine Rosicrucians who come down in their influencing work over the centuries, from the time of the Chymical Wedding of Christian Rosenkreutz, a full relationship to Christ within the Luciferic possibility is already achieved, and Coleridge initially reflects the presence of that influence, though he was greatly diverted in his course. Coleridge's dreams bear witness to a powerful Luciferic vision of the Goddess, but distorted and disturbed, on the one hand by the self-love in which Coleridge remains fixed, the combined result of his frustrated love of Sara Hutchinson and Wordsworth's pitiless rejection, and on the other by the cultural-intellectual identity Coleridge re-assumes in the face of his humiliation, which, seeking to appropriate the experience to itself, falsifies and introduces fear into the spectacle. In Coleridge's dreams, as Hughes points out, the Goddess "seems wholly negative, utterly horrifying. As in:

> *... a most frightful dream of a Woman whose features were blended with darkness catching hold of my right eye and attempting to pull it out—I caught hold of her arm fast—a horrid feel—Wordsworth cried aloud to me hearing my scream—heard his cry and thought it cruel he did not come/but did not wake till his cry was repeated a third time—the woman's name Ebon Ebon Thalud ...*"[23]

In her name, nevertheless, this Woman reveals much of the essential nature of the Goddess "in her rejected (vengeful) phase"[24], as she reverts to her original chaotic powers as Goddess of the Underworld. In that function she is what the world was originally formed from, "the creative womb of the inchoate waters, gradually refining herself into human form, and everywhere tending to be fish-tailed"[25]. She is fully present in this primordial function in the "deep romantic chasm" of Coleridge's "Kubla Khan", as Hughes points out:

> *Here again are the serpents, the giant slimy things that crawl with legs, bottomless springs, underworld seas, eruptive fountains, etc.—flowing into a river who* [sic] *is also a woman with a musical instrument in one hand and snakes in her crown (as in Apuleius' vision of Egyptian Isis).*[26]

In the poem the vision of the Goddess is perfectly mediated and Coleridge himself fully centred, the effect of the positive Rosicrucian influence at work in Coleridge at this time.[27]

Luciferic capability of the kind that Coleridge possessed, in which the inner world has begun to open out on an outer content, and which is to be traced back to Rosicrucian sources, is only carried over into the modern world successfully from within the Rosicrucian Anthroposophical culture. We may see it as a case of the Imagination of Romantic provenance evolving further into pictoriality.[28] Something of the full range of pictoriality that belongs to the evolved Imagination is suggested in exoteric tradition in the vast mythological material that concerns the Goddess, which Robert Graves and Ted Hughes strenuously recovered to view, especially where this material dovetails on the associated actions of the Goddess's Son and Lover who is termed the "Star of Life", and his double and twin, the "Serpent of Wisdom".[29] Graves points out that at a certain point in history, which he relates to the coming of Jesus, "The Serpent [also] had become the Devil".[30] Here indeed is a useful reflection of a large part of the Anthroposophical revelation, insofar as this involves the indispensable roles played in the evolution of the Imagination today by Lucifer and Ahriman, respectively the Star of Life *and* the Serpent of Wisdom, and the Devil who, associated with the Serpent, at a certain point in time makes his own role felt. An extraordinary intuition of *new* possibilities and *new* challenges underlies the extensive mythological research of Graves and Hughes, but, inevitably, the matter is pursued from an historical perspective only, as it were from the outside looking in, for the most part wistfully, if out of a profound intuition. In the Anthroposophical revelation, by contrast, the matter is seen directly from within, as an account of how the Imagination itself unfolds in the context of its further necessary evolution in our time.

V

When Steiner brought forward his Mystery Plays, from 1910 to 1913, he stood in relation to his age rather in the way Benedictus does, who is presented as the *type* of the modern-day Initiate, except that Steiner was possessed of powers that associate him also with the figures of Theodosius and Romanus, whose deeper roles over the course of the Plays are only hinted at. As the mediator of the Anthroposophical revelation in our time, Steiner was making arrangements for a variety of activities that would eventually lead to the establishment (in 1924) of the General Anthroposophical Society, his Plays serving to anticipate, from early on, the more advanced forms of engagement and common commitment that Society would have to embrace. His own unfolding work in Imagination, in the meantime, would offer those around him a tremendous vantage point on the infinite variety of higher forces that now lie open to the creative human spirit, with the inevitable demands such access must bring of clearer insight into the creative tasks that lie ahead.

It is easy to see how resistance to these demands could be great, and Steiner's Plays themselves acknowledge the many forms of resistance that are bound to be put up from the tremendous complexity of the venture, which requires much self-searching, so that Johannes can still pretend to turn away from the imminent prospect, even with the immense progress he has made up to this point:

> *Johannes will not know how spirit*
> *can answer riddles in dark depths of soul.*
> *He will create, will do an artist's work.*
> *Let that be hidden from him, that in him*
> *would look on cosmic heights with conscious vision.*

Denying all that he has gained from his further evolution, Johannes pretends to revert to that form of artistic commitment that would go on working simply with the sensual forms of the sensory world, in a merely individual relation to them. At the other extreme, Capesius—as the one who should "be proclaiming/the *knowledge* of the spirit unto others"—denies being able to translate the content of *his* experience of the spirit-world into concepts that would lay the ground for a more general cultural approach to such an experience:

> *Much more than in creating outer things*
> *the power of the spirit has to lose*
> *itself in words. The words compel one*

*to **understand** the thing perceived; and concepts*
oppose the power of the seer.

The process by which the creation forces are engaged can be (but need not be in the Anthroposophical dispensation) a terrible one, accompanied, by much shifting about and anguished self-questioning—until the breakthrough comes. At this point these forces are Imaginatively taken hold of, coinciding with an experience of inner purification. One takes charge of these forces, first, in the active exercise of pictorial Imagination, through which we are directed as to their moral content. The threat, otherwise, is that these forces will themselves take us over, (and through the influence of Lucifer and Ahriman) take us down with themselves, without our being able to identify them or knowing that we *are* being taken down, which is already the fate of post-modern humanity. The late-nineteenth century, in *its* confused Imaginative way, intuited this tendency to devolution profoundly, sometimes despairing that the whole creation might be lost, as Strindberg does in *Miss Julie*, where the blame for the impending chaos is put squarely on the Mother. In contrast with this, we may consider the fight Hemingway is still putting up against this tendency to devolution in the creation forces, even if he despairs of again accessing an Imaginative control over them (as in "Kilimanjaro"). At a certain level these forces work their way directly into the physical sphere, and it is in an author like Beckett that we begin to comprehend also in what frightful forms they will one day show themselves in this sphere as they work on, on their own, without the Imaginative control over them it now rests with us to exercise in conjunction with the Sophia. By the time we reach Beckett's *Endgame*, the light of Nature's creation has become virtually extinguished, the Goddess appearing in this play as Mother Pegg who could not find what exchange of light with Man She needed, to recover Her creation:

> Clov. *When old Mother Pegg asked you for oil for her lamp and you told her to get out to hell, you knew what was happening, then, no?*
> *You know what she died of Mother Pegg? of darkness.*
> Hamm. *I hadn't any.*
> Clov. *Yes you did.*

Man is falling away, with the creation, for good, the devolution forces having fully taken over; they express themselves now almost strictly through the physical creation that has been left to itself, to erode away. How Man appears and what it may be said he is left with, when ultimately dissociated from Nature, determines the whole extent of Beckett's presentation, but one will find even in it, an implied exhortation to Man to find Himself again. There is nothing but despair, that this can be achieved at all, but what impresses about Beckett's presentation is the way despair *continues*, as itself a form of resistance to ultimate negation.

Suggested Further Reading

By Rudolf Steiner
Knowledge of the Higher Worlds: How is it achieved?
(reprinted as *How to Know Higher Worlds*)

Three Streams in the Evolution of Mankind
(Lecture Cycle)

◆　　　◆　　　◆

By Sergei O. Prokofieff
The Heavenly Sophia and the Being Anthroposophia

◆　　　◆　　　◆

A full list of printed works by Steiner, including his Mystery Plays, is available from:

The Rudolf Steiner Press
Forest Row, Sussex, England

Endnotes

1. See *The Thinking Spirit: Rudolf Steiner and Romantic Theory* (New York: IUniverse, 2007).

2. See *Othello's Sacrifice: Essays on Shakespeare and Romantic Tradition* (Toronto: Guernica, 1996), and *Prospero's Powers: A Short View of Shakespeare's Last Phase* (New York: IUniverse, 2006).

3. See Ted Hughes's Introduction to his *Choice of Coleridge's Verse* (London: Faber, 1996) for a full account of Coleridge's psychic struggle. Opium, it is well-known, Coleridge wrongly thought his way out, and it hurt him greatly both nervously and physically; hence the need to get away to convalesce.

4. See *Prospero's Powers* for my account of this event, pursued in relation to Shakespeare's personal artistic development.

5. Though the matter is not explicitly raised at this point (it will be strongly suggested later), we surmise that, in abandoning the woman who once loved him, Johannes secretly transfers the object of his lustful nature to Maria.

6. For a full treatment of the demonic import of Coleridge's terrifying psychic imagination and his efforts to come to terms, see Ted Hughes's Introduction to his *Choice of Coleridge's Verse*, entitled "The Snake and the Oak".

7. In *The Thinking Spirit*, cited above, my purpose is, precisely, to see the reader through the many, discrete stages of that process, as Steiner's work elaborates on these. The reader will find in the collection of texts I offer from Steiner's work much of the theoretical background (with its roots in Romantic writing) he/she will need, to fill in the contextual import of Steiner's action in his plays.
   The word "strength" is repeated five times in Benedictus's account of Johannes's progress: in the first three instances of the word, the actual thinking power underlying such strength is denoted, in the fourth

instance Johannes's success in coming into such strength, in the fifth the final element of re-inforcing support gratuitously offered by the initiate (in this case, Benedictus) to the candidate who has come this far.

8. For a discussion of Coleridge's distinction between the two imaginative faculties, see Ted Hughes "The Snake and The Oak", cited above, p.9.

9. I intend this as a complex statement. Coleridge wrote the first part of "Christabel" before he met Sara. However, he took up the second part *after* their meeting, and it has been suggested (by Rosemary Ashton in her biography on Coleridge, *The Life of Samuel Taylor Coleridge*, Blackwell, 1996) that after this meeting "it became more impossible than ever for him to handle [his theme] in the poem." (p.185). There is at least that kind of basis for reading Sara into the poem, and an evolution in Coleridge's life-experience that suggests that at a certain point her identification with its theme had become the primal fact.

10. See the Intro to *Coleridge's Verse*, p.95.

11. Hughes's Intro, p.56.

12. See the last pages of Hughes's Intro: his "Postscript", to which he gives the title "The Snake in the Spine", pp.90–96.

13. In his *Women in Love*. Among other things, my purpose in these pages is to question Hughes's too easy championing of what is to be found in "the blood-stream", as if great danger did not lurk there.

14. Coleridge himself quite fully understood that the process of Imagination was not one for "the sensual and the proud" (see "Dejection"); English Romantic Imaginative production at its best is very consciously predicated on this understanding. It is in another respect that the English Romantics fail to take *their* explorations any further. Breaking in magnificently upon these "pure, and in their purest hour" (each in his varied way), the Imagination begins to disclose what can only be described as the inner content of the *outer* world. The *inner* world, remains, for its part, relatively unexplored, and we are as a result still removed from the discovery of an outer content to that world.

15. This is Yeats's position in "Ego Dominuus Tuus" until the later descent into atavism.

16. Such recognition in Capesius takes the form of a Dante-like overcoming of fundamental resistance, based as this is in his consciousness of his glar-

ing inadequacies before the prospect that yawns before him:

And so I recognize the highest duty—
but if I wish to venture the first step
into the realm from which I must not turn,
I feel at once the failure of the powers,
with which my thought, so proudly,
intended to reveal the aims of life...

17. Cf. *The Waste Land*: "We think of the key, each in his prison/Thinking of the key, each confirms a prison/Only at nightfall..."
    Capesius's role as intellectual-cultural hero is acknowledged early on in Steiner's play, by Maria, who, despite her admiration, points the weakness in Capesius's experience:

    That form of spirit, to which I belong,
    sends into deep realities
    the harvest of its words
    because in deep realities
    it wills to plant its roots.
    The writing in the heavens of the spirit
    is from your thinking far remote—
    proclaiming in its solemn letters
    how a new shoot will come
    upon the tree of man.

    Cf. *The Waste Land*:

    What are the roots that clutch, what branches grow
    Out of this stony rubbish? Son of man,
    You cannot say, or guess, for you know only
    A heap of broken images, where the sun beats,
    And the dead tree gives no shelter, the cricket no relief,
    And the dry stone no sound of water.

18. See *The Use of Poetry and The Use of Criticism* (London: Faber and Faber, 1959; orig, pub., 1933), p.69: "But for a few years he had been visited by his Muse (I know of no poet to whom this hackneyed metaphor is better applicable) and thenceforth was a haunted man; for anyone who has ever been visited by the Muse is thenceforth haunted."
    This haunting would become the special focus of Eliot's *Four Quartets* (of "Burnt Norton", most notably), as well as of several of Eliot's later plays.

19. Unconsciously driven by an *earlier* manifestation of the Anthroposophical Spirit, Shakespeare finds himself likewise contending with the seemingly inexpungeable problems of lust or self-love and the more general problem of greed that at a certain level also includes the problem of intellectual over-determination—in forms that are both well-meant (as in the case of Shakespeare's 'good' characters) and ill-meant (in the case of his 'evil' characters). Through his extensive meditations on this wide range of human experience, as dramatized by the characters of his creation, Shakespeare would seem to have been working out his own share in these problems insofar as they continued to determine his own essential human nature. In contrast with the problematic character of the development as dramatized between Johannes and Capesius, there is an indication in Shakespeare at a certain point of a very grand expunging of these inculpating tendencies, which I associate with his unique experience of living *through* the ending of *King Lear*. (See *Othello's Sacrifice*, Part Three).

20. See *The East in the Light of the West* (New York: Anthroposophic Press, 1922), p.119.

21. *The East in the Light of the West*, p.119.

22. *The East in the Light of the West*, p.119.

23. See his "Introduction", p.57.

24. As per Hughes, "Introduction", p.59n.

25. Hughes, p.6.

26. Hughes, p.31.

27. Anthroposophical culture today, among other things, reveals that Christian Rosenkreutz himself forms the subject of Rembrandt's *Polish Rider*, in which painting we find the same elements of presentation as are contained in Coleridge's poem: and so, the overhanging dome, with illuminating sun in the background; the central role of the Rider with whom we compare Kubla and (in the poem's development in the second half) Coleridge, the poet; and, finally, the underground world that appears to be almost giving way beneath Rembrandt's Rider, and out of which come the great fructifying powers of Coleridge's poem. These last have been transposed in Rembrandt's painting to the figure of the Rider himself in whom, along with the powers of the upper and middle spheres, they are so superbly manifested. We shall find these three spheres represented yet

again in Goethe's *Tale of the Green Snake and the Beautiful Lily* (written contemporaneously with Coleridge's "Kubla Khan") in which Steiner has claimed a *direct* influence from the Rosicrucian stream (see his *Theosophy of the Rosicrucian* (London: Rudolf Steiner Press, 1981), pp.8–9).

28. We can also speak of the Imagination as ecstasy, which is also Luciferic in origin and a *prelude* to the pictorial experience: Capesius and Johannes both undergo this preliminary stage. Ecstasy of this sort is as far as Eliot seems to have gone, and he thought he could see in Coleridge's experience, while under the influence of his Muse, a condition which compared directly with his own. What also underlies Coleridge's ecstasy, however, is the horror of the shadow of an outer presence. Eliot can be said at least to look *into* this experience in the peculiar nature of the "haunting" *he* represents both in his poems and his plays. Otherwise, Luciferic ecstasy and Ahrimanic horror are centrally referred, in Eliot, to the reconciling power of the Word: "Here the impossible union/Of spheres of existence is actual"; it is here that these spheres are "conquered and reconciled" (See the *Four Quartets*, "The Dry Salvages").

29. See Robert Graves, *The White Goddess* (New York: Farrar, Straus and Giroux, 1966), pp.387ff.

30. Graves, p.389.

978-0-595-46617-7
0-595-46617-6

www.ingramcontent.com/pod-product-compliance
Lightning Source LLC
Chambersburg PA
CBHW050345290526
45785CB00006B/2644